The Sayings

The Sayings of

LORD
BYRON

selected & introduced by

STODDARD MARTIN

DUCKWORTH

First published in 1990 by
Gerald Duckworth & Co. Ltd.
The Old Piano Factory
43 Gloucester Crescent
London NW1

Introduction and editorial arrangement
© 1990 by Stoddard Martin

ISBN 0 7156 2351 6

British Library Cataloguing in Publication Data
Byron, George Gordon Byron, Baron *1788–1824*
The Sayings of Lord Byron.
1. Poetry in English. Byron, George Gordon
Byron, Baron 1788–1824
I. Title   II. Martin, Stoddard *1948–*
821.7

ISBN 0-7156-2351-6

Photoset in North Wales by
Derek Doyle & Associates, Mold, Clwyd
Printed in Great Britain by
Redwood Press Limited, Melksham

Contents

Introduction

When Lady Caroline Lamb described her lover as 'mad, bad and dangerous to know', she contributed mightily to the myth of Byron as the Lucifer among Romantic poets; but she got it substantially wrong. Compared to contemporaries such as Coleridge and Shelley, Byron was singularly conventional and of *this* world. To his friends he was generous, to his enemies decorous, and only to himself really 'bad'. As for his being 'dangerous to know', this might have been the case for one or two Englishwomen of his class who had the temerity to try to possess him and inveighed against him when they failed. But otherwise, for both sexes, Byron turns out to have been one of the most engaging spirits of his time – indeed, as we know from letters published in this century, its most affable correspondent.

His father, 'Mad Jack', was a soldier who died in debauchery in France when the boy was less than five. His uncle, 'the Wicked Lord Byron', died when he was ten, leaving him the barony and large decaying estates. Brought up by a doting Scots Calvinist mother, young Byron developed an urge to escape all smothering domesticity and religious restriction. At Harrow and Cambridge he was popular for his irreverence, good looks and an athletic daring in defiance of a club-foot which he took as his personal mark of Cain. Always a fatalist, he enjoyed his first happiness as a free spirit, roving the Mediterranean on a 'grand tour' which became at times a sybaritic preview of the twentieth-century hippy's 'journey to the East'. From the record of this, *Childe Harold's Pilgrimage*, he awoke in 1812 to find himself famous; and for the next three years he was pursued by the likes of Caroline Lamb as the lion of literary London.

Byron's was an antithetical nature. 'I was born for opposition,' he said; and, especially in the 'tight little island' of Britain, he was usually *against*: against matriarchal despotism, manipulative 'feminie', Bluestocking taste, the critical establishment, Toryism in

general, Castlereagh and Wellington in particular – the
ancien régime. By contrast, he was *for*: sisters, lovers, free
spirits when not reckless, exuberance in literature, a good
joke, his 'friends the Whigs', freedom from kings
throughout Europe, and his 'poor little pagod' Napoleon.
Liberation, liberty, libertinism – he was a 'liberal' in all
these respects; at the same time, he believed in proper
form. We are told that he was annoyed at Constantinople
when not given an aristocrat's pride of place to view the
Sultan's procession; he lauded Pope as a stylist above all
his contemporaries; he warned his political friends not to
be taken in by more die-hard radicals; and when he left
England for good in 1816 he hurtled across the Continent
in a replica of Napoleon's Imperial coach.

Indolence characterised his life when settled, whether at
his ancestral estate, Newstead Abbey, where he drank out
of a skull-mug and fornicated with the local 'Paphian
goddesses', or at the Palazzo Mocenigo in Venice, where
he kept a menagerie of mastiffs and monkeys and
entertained a procession of prostitutes. The urge to settle
provoked him to the most disastrous decision of his career:
to undertake a 'good', reforming marriage to Caroline
Lamb's prim cousin, Annabella Milbanke. This ended in
recriminations – indeed, *de*formations – so violent that,
after his departure to the Continent, Byron never saw his
wife, his daughter or his homeland again. A more
agreeable type of liaison for him turned out to be the Italian
institution of *cavaliere servente*: the serving as lover to a
high-born married lady, a status he adopted with the
Countess Teresa Guiccioli, his 'last attachment', with
whom he remained for half a dozen years.

But even within this comfortable situation an antithetical
restlessness was bound to rise up and overwhelm his
indolence. Thus after years of dabbling in Italian
revolutionary politics with Teresa's *Carbonari* relatives,
Byron was persuaded to sail to Greece and organise its
fight for independence against the Turk. This fatal
adventure was prefigured in the poet's belief that
'scribbling' was an inferior occupation and that one's life
could only be justified finally by some heroic act: hence the
'manly' Byron, who was always loath to caper in a lady's
chamber too long and lived in large part to impress his
great male correspondents – the poet Tom Moore, the

publisher John Murray, the politician John Cam Hobhouse and others. It was Hobhouse's proposal as director of the London Greek Committee which provoked Byron finally to his last journey; also Shelley's enthusiasm for the Greek leader Mavrocordato during his exile at Pisa. But Byron was already more than eager to play to a politically-attuned audience, even though ill-suited for his role as war-lord. He had grown weary of 'Italian operatics' and of life in general, and was ready for splendid martyrdom.

Byron's death at Missolonghi at the age of thirty-six re-established his status as legend, begun years before when he was the best-selling poet the world had (or ever has) known. The Greeks erected a cult of the liberator around him; and, as recently as 1989, Chinese student insurgents recited his words in Tienanmen Square. Goethe put him in *Faust* as Euphorion, the blithe spirit who expires in a blaze of beauty and daring; and later Romantics from Stendhal to Wilde harked back to him as the prototype of the brooding individualist who realises his destiny despite the forces against him and consumes himself with the intensity of a hard, gem-like flame. But in fact this was only part of the true Byron: the Byron of *The Corsair* and *Lara*: the misanthropic Nietzschean of *Manfred* and other black melodramas written in reaction to his failed marriage and self-enforced wanderings. The real Byron, as he tells us, loved to laugh and was rarely *larmoyant*: he was not the melancholy narcissist of *Childe Harold* so much as the loose and fun-loving rhymester of *Don Juan*.

This great epic, product of his happiest years in Italy, is, as he says, 'the sublime of *that there* sort of writing' – 'full of pastime and prodigality'. With the clouds of his English life removed – all its real and imaginary responsibilities and oppressions – he is free to enjoy the *dolce far niente*, listening to 'that soft bastard Latin', the 'language of musicians', which, as it falls gently on his ear, creates a happier, freer English of its own. And this is the surpassing accomplishment of *Don Juan*: life, liberty and the pursuit of happiness not only in content (for what is this Don's career but an apotheosis of the free spirit?), but also in language and form. In his adopted Italian *ottava rima*, Byron found himself making rhymes, forging juxtapositions, which made him burst out of his writing-chamber splitting his sides with mirth, racing to read the latest to his mistress or minions (Leigh Hunt, for example, whom he supported as editor of *The Liberal* and gave an entire floor of his house) with a tumbler of gin-punch in his hand.

And alongside *Don Juan* were the letters to his friends back home: Hobhouse, Murray, Moore, as mentioned; his financial administrator Douglas Kinnaird, and his half-sister Augusta Leigh (with whom he had an affair which contributed to the demise of his marriage). These letters, like the poem, are the triumph in Byron's nature of lively spirit over morbidity. Self-analytical while far from being self-obsessed – self-lampooning as well as self-justifying – they and the journals of his great Italian period give us a unique insight not only into his 'gigantic and exaggerated' times but also into the psychology of one of its titanic personalities. For along with Bonaparte and Beethoven, Byron stood and stands still as the prime exemplar of the new man of a new age: an age in which man had advanced beyond being the pawn of an external God, with all the moral determinations that implied, and had taken on, for better or worse, the terrible freedom to create glory or disaster for himself: the Romantic man whose only god was his fate and whose only salvation, in the face of decay and death, was his courage, productivity and *bon tempérament*.

Note on the text: owing to the eccentricities of Byron's punctuation, prose quotes are given in the form Peter Quennell used in his 1950 edition of the Letters and Journals, while quotes from *Don Juan* are standardised to the current Penguin edition.

Love

Love, in my humble opinion, is utter nonsense, a mere jargon of compliments, romance, and deceit; now, for my part, had I fifty mistresses, I should in the course of a fortnight, forget them all, and, if by any chance I ever recollected one, should laugh at it as a dream, and bless my stars, for delivering me from the hands of the little mischievous Blind God.   *Letter to his half-sister*, 1804

One must make love mechanically, as one swims. I was once very fond of both, but now as I never swim, unless I tumble in the water, I don't make love till almost obliged, though I fear *that* is not the shortest way out of the troubled waves with which in such accidents we must struggle.
Letter to Lady Melbourne, 1812

I do not believe in the existence of what is called love.   (*Ib.*)

Constancy. Who wants it forsooth, or expects it, after sixteen?   (*Ib.*)

One generally *ends* and *begins* with platonism.   (*Ib.* 1813)

If a man is not contented with a pretty woman, and not only runs after any little country girl he meets with, but absolutely boasts of it; he must not be surprised if others admire that which he knows not how to value.   (*Ib.*)

I have been all my life trying to make someone love me, and never got the sort that I preferred before.   (*Ib.*1814)

I am in amity (the purest, and of course most insipid) with a person; and one condition is, that I am to tell her her faults without reserve. How long do you think such a treaty, fully observed, would endure? I will tell you – five minutes.   (*Ib.*)

A new mistress is nothing to an old friend, the latter can't be replaced in this world, nor, I very much fear, in the next.
Letter to John Cam Hobhouse, 1814

Love in this part of the world [Italy] is no sinecure.
Letter to John Murray, 1816

A woman is virtuous (according to the code) who limits herself to her husband and one lover; those who have two, three, or more, are a little *wild*; but it is only those who are indiscriminately diffuse, and form a low connection ... who are considered as over-stepping the modesty of marriage.   *(Ib.1817)*

There is no convincing a woman here, that she is in the smallest degree deviating from the rule of right or the fitness of things, in having an *Amoroso*: the great sin seems to lie in concealing it.   *(Ib.)*

[My current mistress], to whom I have just translated what I have written on our subject [of love] to you, says – 'If you loved me thoroughly, you would not make so many fine reflections, which are only good *forbirsi i scarpi*', – that is, 'to clean shoes withal'.   *Letter to Thomas Moore, 1817*

I am dull ... for I have fallen in love.
Letter to Hobhouse, 1819

In separation the one who goes away suffers less than the one who stays behind.   *Letter to Teresa Guiccioli, 1819*

Never to feel admiration – and to enjoy myself without giving too much importance to the enjoyment in itself – to feel indifference toward human affairs – contempt for many – but hatred for none, this was the basis of my philosophy. I did not mean to love any more, nor did I hope to receive Love. You have put to flight all my resolutions; now I am all yours; I will become what you wish – perhaps happy in your love, but never at peace again.   *(Ib.)*

You should not have re-awakened my heart, for (at least in my own country) my love has been fatal to those I love – and to myself.   *(Ib.)*

Love. In that word, beautiful in all languages, but most so in yours – *Amor mio* – is comprised my existence here and hereafter.   (*Ib.*)

I am, as I said, in perfect indecision, depending on the *will* of a woman who has none, and on whom I never calculate for more than twelve hours. She will do as she pleases, and then so will I.   *Letter to Douglas Kinnaird, 1819*

A young Italian, married to a rich old Patrician, with only one man besides for a lover, is not likely to embarrass either with a long Constancy.   (*Ib.*)

[Italian women] marry for their parents, and love for themselves. They exact fidelity from a lover as a debt of honour, while they pay the husband as a tradesman, that is, not at all. You hear a person's character, male or female, canvassed, not as depending on their conduct to their husbands or wives, but to their mistress or lover.
   Letter to Murray, 1820

The populace and the women are, as usual, all for those who are in the wrong, viz. the lady and her lover.
   Letter to Moore, 1820

It is awful work, this love, and prevents all a man's projects of good or glory.   (*Ib.* 1821)

All my loves go crazy, and make scenes.
   Letter to his half-sister, 1821

I rather look upon love altogether as a sort of hostile transaction, very necessary to make or to break matches, and keep the world going, but by no means a sinecure to the parties concerned.   *Letter to Lady Hardy, 1822*

I am worn out in feelings ... Though only thirty-six, I feel sixty in mind.   *Conversation with Lady Blessington, 1823*

Don Juan

Oh Love, how perfect is thy mystic art,
Strengthening the weak and trampling on the strong.
How self-deceitful is the sagest part
Of mortals whom thy lure hath led along.   (I.106)

Love's a capricious power. I've known it hold
Out through a fever caused by its own heat,
But be much puzzled by a cough and cold
And find a quinsy very hard to treat.   (II.22)

Oh love, thou art the very god of evil,
For after all, we cannot call thee devil.   (II.205)

Love, constant love, has been my constant guest,
And yet last night, being at a masquerade,
I saw the prettiest creature, fresh from Milan,
Which gave me some sensations like a villain.   (II.209)

… if one sole lady pleased forever,
How pleasant for the heart, as well as liver!   (II.213)

… Let none think to fly the danger,
For soon or late Love is his own avenger.   (IV.73)

… Love is for the free!   (V.127)

… Love is vanity,
Selfish in its beginning as its end,
Except where 'tis a mere insanity …   (IX.73)

The noblest kind of love is love platonical,
To tend or to begin with. The next grand
Is that which may be christened love canonical,
Because the clergy take the thing in hand.
The third sort to be noted in our chronicle
As flourishing in every Christian land
Is when chaste matrons to their other ties
Add what may be called marriage in disguise.   (IX.76)

Now hatred is by far the longest pleasure;
Men love in haste, but they detest at leisure.   (XIII.6)

Women

I do not admire 'that dangerous thing a female wit' ... I despise the sex too much to squabble with them.
Letter to Hobhouse, 1810

I am always but too happy to find a woman to regulate or misregulate me, and I am as docile as a dromedary, and can bear almost as much.   *Letter to Lady Melbourne*, 1812

A woman should never be seen eating or drinking, unless it be *lobster salad* and *champagne*, the only true feminine and becoming viands.   (*Ib.*)

With all my presumed prejudice against your sex, or rather the perversion of manners and principle in many, which you admit in some circles, I think the worst woman that ever existed would have made a man of very passable reputation. They are all better than us, and their faults, such as they are, must originate with ourselves.
Letter to Annabella Milbanke, 1813

There is something to me very softening in the presence of a woman, – some strange influence, even if one is not in love with them – which I cannot at all account for, having no very high opinion of the sex. But yet, – I always feel in better humour with myself and everything else if there is a woman within ken.   *Journal*, 1814

I don't talk – I can't flatter, and won't listen, except to a pretty or a foolish woman.   (*Ib.*)

The more I see of men, the less I like them. If I could but say so of women too, all would be well.   (*Ib.*)

I do not tire of women *personally*, but because they are generally bores in their disposition.
Letter to Murray, 1817

A woman [is] never at a loss [to explain] – the devil always sticks by them.   *Letter to Moore, 1817*

I … am sure that I should have preferred Medea to any woman that ever breathed.   *(Ib. 1818)*

My own dear precious *Amica* … hates all flirting but her own.   *Letter to his half-sister, 1819*

I like women – God he knows – but the more their system here [in Italy] develops upon me, the worse it seems … the *polygamy* is all on the female side. I have been an intriguer, a husband, a whoremonger, and now I am a *cavaliere servente* – by the holy! it is a strange sensation.
                    Letter to Hobhouse, 1819

It is best to let the women alone, in the way of conflict, for they are sure to win against the field.
                    Letter to Moore, 1820

Our age is in everything an affected age, and where affectation prevails the *fair* sex – or rather the *blue* – are always strongly tinctured with it. A little learning may be swelled to an enormous size by artifice … The philosophical petticoats of our times surpass even those of the age of Elizabeth who pretended to cultivate an acquaintance with the classics.   *Letter to Kinnaird, 1820*

I never interfere in any matters with the women or children of my friends. It is the only quiet course.   *(Ib.1821)*

After the life I have led, a *good* opinion is the only rational one which a man should entertain of the whole sex – up to *thirty*, the worst possible opinion a man can have of them in *general*, the better for himself. Afterwards, it is a matter of no importance to *them*, nor to him either, *what opinion* he entertains – his day is over, or, at least, should be.
                    Letter to Richard Hoppner, 1821

Women all over the world always retain their freemasonry, and as that consists in the illusion of the sentiment which constitutes their sole empire (all owing to chivalry and the Goths – the Greeks knew better), all works which refer to the *comedy* of the passions, and laugh at sentimentalism, of course are proscribed by the whole *sect*.

Letter to Hobhouse, 1821

The state of women under the ancient Greeks – convenient enough. Present state a remnant of the barbarism of the chivalric and feudal ages – artificial and unnatural. They ought to mind home – and be well fed and clothed – but not mixed in society. Well educated too, in religion – but to read neither poetry nor politics – nothing but books of piety and cookery. Music – drawing – dancing – also a little gardening and ploughing now and then.   *Diary*, 1821

Be assured from me that a women (as society is constituted in England) who gives any advantage to a man may expect a lover, but will sooner or later find a tyrant; and this is not the man's fault either, perhaps, but is the necessary and natural result of the circumstances of society, which, in fact, tyrannise over the man equally with the woman; that is to say, if either of them have any feeling or honour.

Letter to Lady Hardy, 1822

If I left a woman for another woman, she might have cause to complain, but really when a man merely wishes to go on a great duty, for a good cause, this selfishness on the part of the 'feminie' is rather too much.

Letter to Kinnaird, 1823 (on going to Greece)

There never was a man who gave up so much to women, and all I have gained by it has been the character of treating them harshly.   *(Ib.)*

Don Juan

… I hate a dumpy woman.   (I.61)

A hint in tender cases is enough.
Silence is best; besides there is a tact …
Which keeps, when pushed by questions rather rough,
A lady always distant from the fact.
The charming creatures lie with such a grace,
There's nothing so becoming to the face.   (I.178)

Man's love is of man's life a thing apart
'Tis woman's whole existence ….   (I.194)

A thankless husband, next a faithless lover,
Then dressing, nursing, praying, and all's over …
Few changes e'er can better their affairs,
Theirs being an unnatural situation,
From the dull palace to the dirty hovel.
Some play the devil, and then write a novel.   (II. 200-1)

In her first passion woman loves her lover,
In all the others all she loves is love,
Which grows a habit she can ne'er get over
And fits her loosely like an easy glove …   (III.3)

A woman's teardrop melts, a man's half sears
Like molten lead, as if you thrust a pike in
His heart to force it out, for (to be shorter)
To them 'tis a relief, to us a torture.   (V.118)

A tigress robbed of young, a lioness,
Or any interesting beast of prey,
Are similes at hand for the distress
Of ladies who cannot have their own way.   (V.132)

There is a tide in the affairs of women
'Which taken at the flood leads' – God knows
    where.   (VI.2)

Some reckon women by their suns or years;
I rather think the moon should date the dears.   (X.10)

Think not, fair creatures, that I mean to abuse you all;
I have always liked you better than I state.
Since I've grown moral, still I must accuse you all
Of being apt to talk at a great rate.   (XII.28)

I've seen a virtuous woman put down quite
By the mere combination of a coterie;
Also a so-so matron boldly fight
Her way back to the world by dint of plottery.   (XIII.82)

The earth has nothing like a she-epistle,
And hardly heaven, because it never ends.
I love the mystery of a female missal,
Which like a creed ne'er says all it intends …   (XIII.105)

'Petticoat influence' is a great reproach,
Which even those who obey would fain be thought
To fly from, as from hungry pikes a roach;
But since beneath it upon earth we are brought
By various joltings of life's hackney coach,
I for one venerate a petticoat,
A garment of a mystical sublimity,
No matter whether russet, silk, or dimity.   (XIV.26)

A something all-sufficient for the heart
Is that for which the sex are always seeking,
But how to fill up that same vacant part?
There lies the rub, and this they are but weak in.   (XIV.74)

No friend like to a woman earth discovers,
So that you have not been nor will be lovers.   (XIV.93)

'Tis wonderful how oft the sex have heard
Long dialogues which passed without a word!   (XV.76)

But wear the newest mantle of hypocrisy
On pain of much displeasing the gynocracy.   (XVI.52)

Marriage

I must marry to repair the ravages of myself and prodigal ancestry; but if I am ever so unfortunate as to be presented with an Heir, instead of a *Rattle* he shall be provided with a *Gag*.   *Letter to his half-sister*, 1811

If I can't persuade some wealthy dowdy to ennoble the dirty puddle of her mercantile Blood, – why – I shall leave England and all its clouds for the East again; I am very sick of it already.   (*Ib.*)

As to Lady Byron, when I discover one rich enough to suit me and foolish enough to have me, I will give her leave to make me miserable if she can. Money is the magnet; as to Women, one is as well as another, the older the better, we have then a chance of getting her to Heaven.   (*Ib.*)

As to love, that is done in a week (provided the lady has a reasonable share); besides, marriage goes on better with esteem and confidence than romance, and she [his future wife] is quite pretty enough to be loved by her husband, without being so glaringly beautiful as to attract too many rivals.   *Letter to Lady Melbourne*, 1812

I don't see how a man with a beautiful wife – *his own* children, – quiet – fame – competency and friends … can be offended with any thing.   *Letter to Moore*, 1813

I never see any one much improved by matrimony. All my coupled contemporaries are bald and discontented. Wordsworth and Southey have both lost their hair and good humour; and the last of the two had a good deal to lose. But it don't much signify what falls *off* a man's temples in that state.   *Journal*, 1813

A wife would be my salvation. I am sure the wives of my acquaintances have hitherto done me little good.   (*Ib.*)

I should like to have somebody now and then to yawn with one.   (*Ib.*1814)

I wish I were married, and don't care about beauty, nor *subsequent* virtue – nor much about fortune. I have made up my mind to share the decorations of my betters – but I should like – let me see – liveliness, gentleness, cleanliness, and something of comeliness – and *my own* first born. Was ever a man more moderate?   *Letter to Lady Melbourne*, 1814

My wife, if she had common sense, would have more power over me than any other whatsoever, for my heart always alights on the nearest *perch* – if it is withdrawn it goes God knows where – but one must like something.   (*Ib.*)

As Moore says, 'A pretty wife is something for the fastidious vanity of a *roué* to *retire* upon.'   (*Ib.*)

If you wouldn't mind my words, we shall get on very well together.   *Conversation with his wife*, 1815

One good thing in my marriage is that it will deliver me from my friends.   (*Ib.*)

Good God, I am surely in Hell!   (*Ib.*)

I am listening to that monologue of my father-in-law which he is pleased to call conversation.   *Letter to Hobhouse*, 1815

Swift says 'no *wise* man ever married'; but, for a fool, I think it the most ambrosial of all possible future states. I still think one ought to marry upon *lease*; but am very sure I should renew mine at the expiration, though next term were for ninety and nine years.   *Letter to Moore*, 1815

What a fool was I to marry – and *you* not very wise – my dear – we might have lived so single and so happy – as old maids and bachelors.   *Letter to his half-sister*, 1816

Between metaphysics, mountains, lakes, love unextinguishable, thoughts unutterable, and the nightmare of my own delinquencies, I should, many a good day, have blown my brains out, but for the recollection that it would have given pleasure to my mother-in-law.   *Letter to Moore*, 1817

I have seen some ancient figures of eighty pointed out as *Amorosi* of forty, fifty, and sixty years' standing. I can't say I have ever seen a husband and wife so coupled.   *(Ib.)*

Curran said to Moore – 'so – I hear – you have married a pretty woman – and a very good creature too – an excellent creature – pray – um – *how do you pass your evenings?*' it is a devil of a question that, and perhaps as easy to answer with a wife as with a mistress; but surely they are longer than the nights. I am all for morality now, and shall confine myself henceforward to the strictest adultery, which you will please recollect is all that virtuous wife of mine has left me.   *Letter to Hoppner*, 1819

The tears of a woman who has left her husband for a man, and the weakness of one's own heart, are paramount to [all other] projects.   *Letter to Moore*, 1821

I would rather *not* [re-marry] – thinking it the way to hate each other – for all people whatsoever.
                    Letter to his half-sister, 1821

Ah! it comes too late; it is like telling a man to beware of his wife after he has married her.
                    Conversation on being warned not to go to Greece, 1823

I am convinced of the happiness of domestic life. No man on earth respects a virtuous woman more than I do, and the prospect of retirement in England with my wife and daughter, gives me an idea of happiness I have never experienced before. Retirement will be everything to me, for heretofore my life has been like the ocean in a storm.
                    Conversation reported on his deathbed, 1824

Don Juan

What men call gallantry, and gods adultery,
Is much more common where the climate's sultry.   (I.63)

'Tis melancholy and a fearful sign
Of human frailty, folly, also crime,
That love and marriage rarely can combine,
Although they both are born in the same clime.   (III.5)

… passion in a lover's glorious,
But in a husband is pronounced uxorious.   (III.6)

Think you, if Laura had been Petrarch's wife,
He would have written sonnets all his life?   (III.8)

Wives in their husbands' absences grow subtler,
And daughters sometimes run off with the butler.   (III.21)

To no men are such cordial greetings given
As those whose wives have made them fit for heaven.
                                                (V.154)

… that moral centaur, man and wife.   (V.158)

But in old England when a young bride errs,
Poor thing, Eve's was a trifling case to hers.   (XII.64)

I've also seen some wives (not to forget
The marriage state, the best or worst of any)
Who were the very paragons of wives,
Yet made the misery of at least two lives.   (XIV.95)

Love's riotous, but marriage should have quiet,
And being consumptive, live on a milk diet.   (XV.41)

Philosophy & Religion

I have learnt to philosophise in my travels; and if I had not, complaint was useless.   *Letter to his mother*, 1809

Our first duty is not to do evil; but alas! that is impossible: our next is to repair it, if in our power. *(Ib.*1810)

I begin to find out that nothing but virtue will do in this damned world. I am tolerably sick of vice, which I have tried in its agreeable varieties, and mean, on my return, to cut all my dissolute acquaintance, leave off wine and carnal company, and betake myself to politics and decorum. I am very serious and cynical, and a good deal disposed to moralise; but fortunately for you the coming homily is cut off by default of pen and defection of paper.
Letter to Francis Hodgson, 1810

They say 'Virtue is its own reward', – it certainly should be paid well for its trouble.   *Journal*, 1813

The respectable Job says, 'Why should a *living man* complain?' I really don't know, except it be that a *dead man* can't.   *(Ib.)*

I like … a good hater.   *(Ib.)*

I like energy – even animal energy – of all kinds.   *(Ib.)*

The word 'sensibility' … it seems, is to be an excuse for all kinds of discontent.   *(Ib.)*

I have no conception of any existence which duration would not render tiresome … Eternity won't be the less agreeable or more horrible because one did not expect it. In the mean time, I am grateful for some good, and tolerably patient under certain evils – *grace à Dieu et mon bon tempérament.*   *(Ib.)*

I wonder how the deuce any body could make such a
world; for what purpose dandies, for instance, were
ordained – and kings – and fellows of colleges – and
women of 'a certain age' – and many men of any age – and
myself, most of all!   *(Ib.)*

When one subtracts from life infancy (which is vegetation)
– sleep, eating, and swilling – buttoning and unbuttoning –
how much remains of downright existence? The summer
of a dormouse.   *(Ib.)*

Is there any thing beyond? – *who* knows? *He* that can't tell.
Who tells that there *is*? He who don't know. And when
shall he know? perhaps, when he don't expect, and
generally when he don't wish it. In this last respect,
however, all are not alike; it depends a good deal upon
education, – something upon nerves and habits – but most
upon digestion.   *(Ib.1814)*

The worst of it is I *do* believe!
Conversation with his wife, 1815

Ugly as virtue.   *Letter to Moore*, 1816

As to the future, I never anticipate – '*Carpe diem*' – the past
at least is one's own, which is one reason for making sure
of the present.   *Letter to Murray*, 1817

Fortune, to be sure, is a female, but not such a b * * as the
rest (always excepting your wife and my sister from such
sweeping terms); for she generally has some justice in the
long run. I have no spite against her, though between her
and Nemesis I have had some sore gauntlets to run – but
then I have done my best to deserve no better.
Letter to Moore, 1817

When a man talks of system, his case is hopeless.
(Ib.1818; about Leigh Hunt)

As to the trash about *honour*, that is all stuff; a man offends,
you want to kill him, this is amiable and natural, but *how*?
The natural mode is obvious, but the artificial varies
according to education.   *Letter to Hobhouse*, 1819

An old woman at Rome, reading Boccaccio, exclaimed, 'I wish to God that this was saying one's prayers.'   (*Ib.*)

You may tell a man that he is thought libertine, profligate, a villain, but not that his nose wants blowing or that his neckcloth is ill tied.   *Letter to Alexander Scott, 1819*

To my extreme mortification I grow wiser every day.
                              Letter to Captain John Hay, 1819

The Cant is so much stronger than the *, nowadays, that the benefit of experience in a man who had well weighed the worth of both monosyllables must be lost to despairing posterity.   *Letter to Kinnaird, 1819*

I have quite lost all personal interest about anything except money to supply my own indolent expenses; and when I rouse up to appear to take an interest about anything, it is a temporary irritation like Galvanism upon Mutton.
                              Letter to Hobhouse, 1820

Out of chaos God made a world, and out of high passions comes a people.   *Diary, 1821*

Difficulties are the hotbeds of high spirits, and Freedom the mother of the few virtues incident to human nature.   (*Ib.*)

I should almost regret that my own affairs went well, when those of nations are in peril. If the interests of mankind could be essentially bettered (particularly of these oppressed Italians), I should not so much mind my own 'sma peculiar'. God grant us all better times, or more philosophy!   (*Ib.*)

What Hope is there without a deep leaven of Fear?   (*Ib.*)

If it were not for Hope, where would the Future be? – in hell.   (*Ib.*)

I look upon [Roman Catholicism] as the best religion, as it is assuredly the oldest of the various branches of Christianity.   *Letter to Hoppner, 1821*

I had always thought that a degree of Simplicity was an ingredient of Greatness. *Detached Thoughts*, 1821

If I had to live over again, I do not know what I would change in my life, unless it were *for not to have lived at all*. All history and experience, and the rest, teaches us that the good and evil are pretty equally balanced in this existence, and that what is most to be desired is an easy passage out of it. *(Ib.)*

A material resurrection seems strange, and even absurd, except for purposes of punishment; and all punishment, which is to *revenge* rather than *correct*, must be *morally wrong*. *(Ib.)*

I am always most religious upon a sun-shiny day; as if there was some association between an internal approach to greater light and purity, and the kindler of this dark lanthorn of our eternal existence. *(Ib.)*

What a strange thing is the propagation of life! A bubble of Seed which may be split in a whore's lap – or in the orgasm of a voluptuous dream – might (for aught we know) have formed a Caesar or a Buonaparte: there is nothing remarkable recorded of their Sires, that I know of. *(Ib.)*

A bargain, even between brethren, is a declaration of war. *Letter to Kinnaird*, 1821

Documents ... are the wordly resources of suspicious people. *Letter to Lady Byron*, 1821

People who are never to meet ... may preserve perhaps the courtesies of life, and much of its kindness ... more easily than nearer connections. *(Ib.)*

As long as I retain my feeling and my passion for Nature, I can partly soften or subdue my other passions and resist or endure those of others. *Letter to Isaac d'Israeli*, 1822

[Christian bigots] always forget Christ in their Christianity. *Letter to Murray*, 1822

I think people can never have *enough* of religion, if they are to have any. *Letter to Moore*, 1822

I have ever found that those I liked longest and best, I took to at first sight.   *(Ib.* 1823)

Whenever I see a real Christian, either in practice or in theory, (for I never yet found the man who could produce either, when put to the proof,) I am his disciple. But, till then, I cannot truckle to the tithe-mongers.   *(Ib.)*

Don Juan

Oh Plato, Plato, you have paved the way
With your confounded fantasies to more
Immoral conduct by the fancied sway
Your system feigns o'er the controlless core
Of human hearts than all the long array
Of poets and romancers. You're a bore,
A charlatan, a coxcomb, and have been
At best no better than a go-between.   (I.116)

There's nought no doubt so much the spirit calms
As rum and true religion …   (II.34)

My altars are the mountains and the ocean,
Earth, air, stars – all that springs from the great Whole,
Who hath produced and will receive the soul.   (III.104)

To feel for none is the true social art
Of the world's stoics – men without a heart.   (V.25)

Believe the Jews, those unbelievers, who
Must be believed, though they believe not you.   (V.62)

… I love wisdom more than she loves me.
My tendency is to philosophize
On most things from a tyrant to a tree,
But still the spouseless virgin Knowledge flies.   (VI.63)

When we know what all are, we must bewail us,
But ne'ertheless I hope it is no crime
To laugh at all things, for I wish to know
What after all are all things – but a show?   (VII.2)

I say no more than has been said in Dante's
Verse and by Solomon and by Cervantes,
By Swift, by Machiavel, by Rochefoucault,
By Fenelon, by Luther, and by Plato,
By Tillotson and Wesley and Rousseau,
Who knew this life was not worth a potato.   (VII.3–4)

Ecclesiastes said that all is vanity;
Most modern preachers say the same or show it
By their examples of true Christianity.
In short all know or very soon may know it;
And in this scene of all-confessed inanity,
By saint, by sage, by preacher, and by poet,
Must I restrain me through the fear of strife
From holding up the nothingness of life?   (VII.6)

For me, I sometimes think that life is death,
Rather than life a mere affair of breath.   (IX.16)

It is a pleasant voyage perhaps to float
Like Pyrrho on a sea of speculation.
But what if carrying sail capsize the boat?
Your wise men don't know much of navigation.   (IX.18)

For ever and anon comes indigestion
(Not the most 'dainty Ariel') and perplexes
Our soarings with another sort of question.   (XI.3)

The truth is, I've grown lately rather phthisical.
I don't know what the reason is – the air
Perhaps; but as I suffer from the shocks
Of illness, I grow much more orthodox.   (XI.5)

Be hypocritical, be cautious, be
Not what you seem, but always what you see.   (XI.86)

… I may stand alone,
But would not change my free thoughts for a throne.
                                        (XI.90)

Death, so called, is a thing which makes men weep,
And yet a third of life is passed in sleep.   (XIV.3)

In play there are two pleasures for your choosing:
The one is winning and the other losing.   (XIV.12)

Let no man grumble when his friends fall off,
As they will do like leaves at the first breeze.
When your affairs come round, one way or t'other,
Go to the coffeehouse and take another.   (XIV.48)

Of all the horrid, hideous notes of woe,
Sadder than owl-songs or the midnight blast
Is that portentous phrase, 'I told you so',
Uttered by friends, those prophets of the past.   (XIV.50)

Shut up the world at large, let Bedlam out,
And you will be perhaps surprised to find
All things pursue exactly the same route
As now with those of *soi-disant* sound mind.   (XIV.84)

All present life is but an interjection,
An 'oh!' or 'ah!' of joy or misery
Or a 'ha, ha!' or 'bah!' a yawn or 'pooh!'
Of which perhaps the latter is most true.   (XV.1)

The grand antithesis to the great ennui ...   (XV.2)

Between two worlds life hovers like a star
'Twixt night and morn upon the horizon's verge.
How little do we know that which we are!
How less what we may be! The eternal surge
Of time and tide rolls on and bears afar
Our bubbles. As the old burst, new emerge,
Lashed from the foam of ages; while the graves
Of empires heave but like some passing waves.   (XV.99)

Politics & War

Liberty. I talk in raptures of that *Goddess* because my amiable Mama was so despotic.

Letter to his half-sister, 1805

The maintenance and well-doing of the industrious poor is an object of greater consequence to the community than the enrichment of a few monopolists ... I have seen the state of these miserable men, and it is a disgrace to a civilised country.

Letter to Lord Holland, 1812

My parliamentary schemes are not much to my taste – I spoke twice last Session, and was told it was well enough; but I hate the thing altogether, and have no intention to 'strut another hour' on that stage.

Letter to his half-sister, 1813

I don't know what liberty means, – never having seen it, – but wealth is power all over the world; and as a shilling performs the duty of a pound (besides sun and sky and beauty for nothing) in the East, – *that* is the country.

Journal, 1813

Balance of Europe – posing straws upon kings' noses, instead of wringing them off! Give me a republic, or a despotism of one, rather than the mixed government of one, two, three. *(Ib.)*

I have simplified my politics into an utter detestation of all existing governments; and, as it is the shortest and most agreeable and summary feeling imaginable, the first moment of an universal republic would convert me into an advocate for single and uncontradicted despotism.

(Ib. 1814)

I shall adhere to my party, because it would not be
honourable to act otherwise; but, as to *opinions*, I don't
think politics *worth* an *opinion*. *Conduct* is another thing: – if
you begin with a party, go on with them. I have no
consistency, except in politics; and *that* probably arises
from my indifference on the subject altogether.   (*Ib.*)

Napoleon! ... – how should he, who knows mankind well,
do other than despise and abhor them?   (*Ib.*)

Ah! my poor little pagod, Napoleon, has walked off his
pedestal. He has abdicated, they say ... I cannot bear such a
crouching catastrophe. I must stick to Sylla, for my modern
favourites don't do, – their resignations are of a different
kind.   *Letter to Moore*, 1814

'Yes, my lord ... Bonaparte is in full retreat towards Paris.'
   'I am damned sorry for it. I didn't know but I might live
to see Lord Castlereagh's head on a pole. But I suppose I
shan't, now.'   *Conversation on hearing of Waterloo*

I am sick at heart of politics and slaughters; and the luck
which Providence is pleased to lavish upon Lord
Castlereagh is only a proof of the little value the gods set
upon prosperity, when they permit such * * *s as he and
that drunken corporal, old Blücher, to bully their betters.
                              Letter to Moore, 1815

It is useless to send to the *Foreign Office*: nothing arrives to
me by that conveyance. I suppose some zealous clerk
thinks it a Tory duty to prevent it.   *Letter to Murray*, 1817

There is no freedom in Europe – that's certain; it is besides
a worn-out portion of the globe.   *Letter to Hobhouse*, 1819

My taste for revolution is abated, with my other passions.
                                         (*Ib.*)

I know that revolutions are not to be made with rose water,
but though some blood may, and must be shed on such
occasions, there is no reason it should be *clotted*; in short,
the Radicals seem to be no better than Jack Cade or Wat
Tyler, and to be dealt with accordingly.   (*Ib.*1820)

I see the good old King [George III] is gone to his place: one can't help being sorry, though blindness, and age, and insanity, are supposed to be drawbacks on human felicity; but I am not at all sure that the latter, at least, might not render him happier than any of his subjects.

Letter to Murray, 1820

If we must have a tyrant, let him at least be a gentleman who has been bred to the business, and let us fall by the axe and not by the butcher's cleaver. (*Ib.*)

I shall never be deterred from a duty of humanity by all the assassins of Italy, and that is a wide word. (*Ib.*)

My liberal principles ... (although I do not preach them) are known, and were known when it was far less reputable to be a friend to liberty than it is now.

Letter to Kinnaird, 1820

I do not ... write me down a contributor to the English radical societies, yet wherever I find a poor man suffering for his opinions ... I always let him have a shilling out of a guinea. (*Ib.*1821)

No tyrant nor tyranny nor barbarian army shall make me change my tone or thoughts or notions, or alter anything but my temper. (*Ib.*)

The king-times are fast finishing. There will be blood shed like water, and tears like mist; but the peoples will conquer in the end. I shall not live to see it, but I foresee it.

Diary, 1821

It is difficult to say whether hereditary right, or popular choice, produce the worse Sovereigns ... It is still more difficult to say which form of Government is the *worst* – all are so bad. As for democracy, it is the worst of the whole; for what is (*in fact*) democracy? an Aristocracy of Blackguards.

Detached Thoughts, 1821

Neither house [of Parliament] ever struck me with more
awe or respect than the same number of Turks in a Divan,
or of Methodists in a barn would have done ... Cicero
himself, and probably the Messiah, could never have
alter'd the vote of a single Lord of the Bedchamber or
Bishop.   *(Ib.)*

There is *no* freedom, even for *Masters*, in the midst of
slaves.   *(Ib.)*

As to *political* slavery – so general – it is man's own fault; if
they *will* be slaves, let them!   *(Ib.)*

I remember seeing Blücher in the London Assemblies, and
never saw anything of his age less venerable. With the
voice and manners of a recruiting Sergeant, he pretended
to the honours of a hero; just as if a stone could be
worshipped, because a Man had stumbled over it.   *(Ib.)*

We live in gigantic and exaggerated times, which make all
under Gog and Magog appear pigmean.
                                       Letter to Sir Walter Scott, 1822

It is necessary, in the present clash of philosophy and
tyranny, to throw away the scabbard. I know it is against
fearful odds; but the battle must be fought; and it will be
eventually for the good of mankind, whatever it may be for
the individual who risks himself.   *Letter to Moore*, 1822

Don Juan

I want a hero, an uncommon want,
When every year and month sends forth a new one,
Till after cloying the gazettes with cant,
The age discovers he is not the true one.   (I.1)

'Let there be light,' said God, and there was light!
'Let there be blood,' says man, and there's a sea!   (VII.41)

The drying up a single tear has more
Of honest fame than shedding seas of gore.   (VIII.3)

… 'God save the king' and kings!
For if he don't, I doubt if men will longer.
I think I hear a little bird, who sings
The people by and by will be the stronger …
Then comes the tug of war; 'twill come again
I rather doubt and I would fain say 'fie on't',
If I had not perceived that revolution
Alone can save the earth from hell's pollution.   (VIII.50-1)

For I will teach, if possible, the stones
To rise against earth's tyrants. Never let it
Be said that we still truckle unto thrones.
But ye, our children's children, think how we
Showed what things were before the world was free.

(VIII.135)

Oh Wellington! (Or 'Vilainton', for Fame
Sounds the heroic syllables both ways.)
France could not even conquer your great name,
But punned it down to this facetious phrase – …
Though Britain owes (and pays you too) so much,
Yet Europe doubtless owes you greatly more.
You have repaired Legitimacy's crutch,
A prop not quite so certain as before …
Never had mortal man such opportunity,
Except Napoleon, or abused it more.
You might have freed fallen Europe from the unity
Of tyrants and been blest from shore to shore.   (IX.1–9)

[I] would much rather have a sound digestion
Than Buonaparte's cancer. Could I dash on
Through fifty victories to shame or fame,
Without a stomach what were a good name?   (IX.14)

For me, I deem an absolute autocrat
Not a barbarian, but much worse than that.   (IX.23)

And I will war at least in words (and should
My chance so happen – deeds) with all who war
With thought; and of thought's foes by far most rude,
Tyrants and sycophants have been and are.   (IX.24)

It is not that I adulate the people.
Without me, there are demagogues enough.
And infidels to pull down every steeple
And set up in their stead some proper stuff.
… I wish men to be free
As much from mobs as kings – from you as me.   (IX.25)

Where's Brummell? Dished. Where's Long Pole Wellesley?
  Diddled.
Where's Whitbread? Romilly? Where's George the Third?
Where is his will? That's not so soon unriddled.
And where is 'Fum' the Fourth, our 'royal bird'? …   (XI.77)

I have seen Napoleon, who seemed quite a Jupiter,
Shrink to a Saturn. I have seen a duke
(No matter which) turn politician stupider,
If that can well be, than his wooden look.   (XI.83)

Who hold the balance of the world? Who reign
O'er congress, whether royalist or liberal?
Who rouse the shirtless patriots of Spain,
That make old Europe's journals squeak and gibber all?
Who keep the world, both old and new, in pain
Or pleasure? Who make politics run glibber all?
The shade of Bonaparte's noble daring?
Jew Rothschild and his fellow Christian Baring.   (XII.5)

Poetry & Contemporaries

Scribbling [is] a disease I hope myself cured of.

Letter to his mother, 1811

The time seems past when (as Dr Johnson said) a man was certain to 'hear the truth from his bookseller', for you have paid me so many compliments, that, if I was not the veriest scribbler on earth, I should feel affronted.

Letter to his publisher, 1811

Instruct Mr Murray not to allow his shopman to call the work *Child of Harrow's Pilgrimage*!!!!! as he has done to some of my astonished friends, who wrote to inquire after my *sanity* on the occasion, as well they might.

Letter to R.C. Dallas, 1811

Madame de Staël … hath published an Essay against Suicide, which, I presume, will make somebody shoot himself; – as a sermon by Blenkinsop, in *proof* of Christianity, sent a hitherto most orthodox acquaintance of mine out of a chapel of ease a perfect atheist.

Letter to Moore, 1813

Madame de Staël … is, of course, what all mothers must be, – but will, I venture to prophesy, do what few mothers could – write an Essay upon it. She cannot exist without a grievance – and somebody to see, or read, how much grief becomes her.   *(Ib.)*

Mrs *Stale* – as John Bull may be pleased to denominate Corinne.   *(Ib.)*

All convulsions end with me in rhyme.   *(Ib.)*

I take up books, and fling them down again. I began a comedy, and burnt it because the scene ran into *reality*; – a novel, for the same reason. In rhyme, I can keep more away from facts.   *Journal,* 1813

What is a work – any – or every work – but a desert with fountains, and, perhaps, a grove or two in every day's journey? *(Ib.)*

I have burnt my *Roman* – as I did the first scenes and sketch of my comedy – and, for aught I see, the pleasure of burning is quite as great as that of printing. *(Ib.)*

I have no great esteem for poetical persons, particularly women; they have so much of the 'ideal' in *practics*, as well as *ethics*. *(Ib.)*

[Leigh] Hunt is an extraordinary character, and not exactly of the present age. He reminds me more of the Pym and Hampden times – much talent, great independence of spirit and an austere, yet not repulsive, aspect … He is the bigot of virtue … He is [also] a little opinionated, as all men who are the *centre* of *circles*, wide or narrow – the Sir Oracles, in whose name two or three are gathered together – must be, and as even Johnson was. *(Ib.)*

I detest Petrarch so much, that I would not be the man even to have obtained his Laura, which the metaphysical, whining dotard never could. *(Ib.)*

Madame de Staël … I admire her abilities, but really her society is overwhelming – an avalanche that buries one in glittering nonsense – all snow and sophistry. *(Ib.1814)*

If I have a wife, and that wife has a son – by any body – I will bring up mine heir in the most anti-poetical way – make him a lawyer, or a pirate, or – any thing. But, if he writes too, I shall be sure he is none of mine, and cut him off with a Bank token. *(Ib.)*

At present I am what they call popular as an author – it enables me to serve one or two people without embarrassing anything but my brains – for I never have, nor shall avail myself of the *lucre*.

Letter to Lady Melbourne, 1814

I ... am not much interested in any criticisms, favourable or otherwise. I have had my day, have done with all that stuff; and must try something new – politics – or rebellion – or Methodism – or gaming. Of the last two I have serious thoughts.   *(Ib.)*

As to Mme. de Staël, I never go near her; her books are very delightful, but in society I see nothing but a plain woman forcing one to listen, and look at her, with her pen behind her ear, and her mouth full of ink – so much for her.   *(Ib.)*

I have lately begun to think my things have been strangely over-rated; and, at any rate, whether or not, I have done with them for ever.   *Letter to Moore*, 1814

My great comfort is, that the temporary celebrity I have wrung from the world has been in the very teeth of all opinions and prejudices.   *(Ib.)*

Half of these Scotch and Lake troubadours, are spoilt by living in little circles and petty societies. London and the world is the only place to take the conceit out of a man.   *(Ib.)*

As for poesy, mine is the *dream* of my sleeping Passions; when they are awake, I cannot speak their language, only in their Somnambulism, and just now they are not dormant.   *Letter to Murray*, 1817

Voltaire has asked *why* no woman has ever written even a tolerable tragedy? 'Ah (said the Patriarch) the composition of a tragedy requires ∗ ∗ ∗.' If this be true, Lord knows what Joanna Baillie does; I suppose she borrows them.   *(Ib.)*

I won't quarrel with the public, however, for the 'Bulgars' are generally right.   *Letter to Moore*, 1818

With regard to the Poeshie, I will have no 'cutting and slashing' … Don Juan shall be an entire horse, or none.
Letter to Hobhouse and Kinnaird, 1819

As to the prudery of the present day … Is there anything in 'Don Juan' so strong as in Ariosto, or Voltaire, or Chaucer?   (*Ib.*)

Whatever brain-money you get on my account from Murray, pray remit me. I will never consent to pay away what I *earn*. That is *mine*, and what I get by my brains I will spend * * *, as long as I have a tester or a * remaining. I shall not live long, and for that reason I must live while I can.   (*Ib.*)

You ask me for the plan of Donny Johnny: I *have* no plan – I *had* no plan. … Why, Man, the Soul of such writing is its licence.
Letter to Murray, 1819

Do you suppose that I could have any intention but to giggle and make giggle?   (*Ib.*)

'Don Juan' … is the sublime of *that there* sort of writing – it may be bawdy but is it not good English? It may be profligate but is it not *life*, is it not *the thing*? Could any man have written it who has not lived in the world? – and [t]ooled in a post-chaise? – in a hackney coach? – in a gondola? – against a wall? – in a court carriage? – in a vis à vis? – on a table? – and under it?   *Letter to Kinnaird*, 1819

The reading or non-reading a book will never keep down a single petticoat.
Letter to Hoppner, 1819

I am tired of scribbling, and nothing but the convenience of an occasional extra thousand pounds would have induced me to go on.
Letter to Hobhouse, 1820

My opinions on my poeshie are always those of the last person I hear speak about them.   (*Ib.*)

For my own part I don't understand a word of the whole four cantos [of his poem on Dante], and was therefore lost in admiration of their sublimity.   *(Ib.)*

Mr Keats, whose poetry you enquire after, appears to me what I have already said: such writing is a sort of mental masturbation – ******** his Imagination. I don't mean he is *indecent*, but viciously soliciting his own ideas into a state, which is neither poetry nor any thing else but a Bedlam vision produced by raw pork and opium.

Letter to Murray, 1820

Don't be afraid of praising me too highly. I shall pocket my blushes.   *Letter to Moore,* 1820

[Writing] comes over me in a kind of rage every now and then, like ****, and then, if I don't write to empty my mind, I go mad. As to that regular, uninterrupted love of writing … I do not understand it. I feel it as a torture, which I must get rid of, but never as a pleasure. On the contrary, I think composition a great pain.   *(Ib.*1821)

You see what it is to throw pearls to swine. As long as I wrote the exaggerated nonsense which has corrupted the public taste, they applauded to the very echo, and, now that I have really composed, within these three or four years, some things which should 'not willingly be let die', the whole herd snort and grumble and return to wallow in their mire. However, it is fit I should pay the penalty of spoiling them, as no man has contributed more than me in my earlier compositions to produce that exaggerated and false taste.   *Letter to Isaac d'Israeli,* 1820

Fielding [is] the *prose* Homer of human nature.

Diary, 1821

I have met with most poetry upon trunks [as lining]; so that I am apt to consider the trunk-maker as the sexton of authorship.   *(Ib.)*

I have read all W. Scott's novels at least fifty times ... [He is the] Scotch Fielding, as well as great English poet – wonderful man! I long to get drunk with him.   (*Ib.*)

Hazlitt ... *talks pimples* – a red and white corruption rising up (in little imitation of mountains upon maps), but containing nothing, and discharging nothing, except their own humours.   (*Ib.*)

I will show more *imagery* in twenty lines of Pope than in any equal length of quotation in English poesy ... There is hardly a line from which a *painting* might not be made, and is.   *Letter to Murray*, 1821

You know my high opinion of your own poetry, – because it is of *no* school.   *Letter to Percy Bysshe Shelley*, 1821

You want me to undertake a great poem – I have not the inclination nor the power. As I grow older, the indifference – *not* to life, for we love it by instinct – but to the stimuli of life, increases.   (*Ib.*)

In general, I do not draw well with literary men: not that I dislike them, but I never know what to say to them after I have praised their last publication. There are several exceptions, to be sure; but then they have either been men of the world, such as Scott, and Moore, etc., or visionaries out of it, such as Shelley.   *Detached Thoughts*, 1821

I have more than once heard Sheridan say, that he never 'had a shilling of his own': to be sure, he contrived to extract a good many of other people's.   (*Ib.*)

One of my notions, different from those of my contemporaries, is, that the present is not a high age of English Poetry: there are *more* poets (soi-disant) than ever there were, and proportionally *less* poetry.   (*Ib.*)

Francis I wrote, after the battle of Pavia, 'All is lost except our honour.' A hissed author may reverse it – '*Nothing* is lost, except our honour.'   *Letter to Moore*, 1821

I do not think Shakespeare without the grossest of faults.
Letter to Octavius Gilchrist, 1821

I look upon a proper appreciation of Pope as a touchstone of taste.   (*Ib.*)

I do not deny the natural powers of Mind of the courtier dramatists, but I think that their service as a *standard* is doing irreparable mischief.   (*Ib.*)

If I ever *do* return to England (which I shan't though), I will write a poem to which *English Bards*, etc., shall be New Milk, in comparison. Your present literary world of moutebanks stands in need of such an Avatar; but I am not yet quite bilious enough: a season or two more, and a provocation or two, will wind me up to the point, and then, have at the whole set!   *Letter to Murray*, 1821

The pity of these men [the leading London writers of the day] is, that they never lived either in *high life*, nor in *solitude*: there is no medium for the knowledge of the *busy* or the *still* world. If admitted into high life for a season, it is merely as *spectators* – they form no part of the Mechanism thereof.   (*Ib.*)

Send me *no* opinions whatsoever, either *good*, *bad*, or *indifferent*, of yourself, or your friends, or others, concerning any work, or works, of mine, past, present, or to come.   (*Ib.*)

Reviews and Magazines are at the best but ephemeral and superficial reading: *who thinks* of the *grand article* of *last year* in any *given review*? ... If they regard *myself*, they tend to increase *Egotism*; if favourable, I do not deny that the praise *elates*, and if unfavourable, that the abuse *irritates*.   (*Ib.*)

Like all imaginative men, I, of course, embody myself with the character while I *draw* it, but not a moment after the pen is from off the paper.   *Letter to Moore*, 1822

As to poor Shelley ... he is, to my knowledge, the *least* selfish and the mildest of men – a man who has made more sacrifices of his fortune and feelings for others than any I ever heard of. With his speculative opinions I have nothing in common, nor desire to have. (*Ib.*)

Poor Shelley! ... how we used to laugh now and then, at various things, which are grave in the Suburbs!
Letter to Murray, 1822

You are all mistaken about Shelley. You do not know how mild, how tolerant, how good he was in Society; and as perfect a Gentleman as ever crossed a drawing-room, when he liked, and where he liked. (*Ib.*)

As for my 'Works' ... let them go to the Devil, from whence (if you believe many persons) they came.
Letter to Alfred d'Orsay, 1823

There is no sovereign in the republic of letters; and even if there were, I have never had the pretension or the power to become a usurper. *Letter to J.J. Coulmann*, 1823

Poetry should only occupy the idle. In more serious affairs it would be ridiculous.
Conversation with Lady Blessington, 1823

Don Juan

Thou shalt believe in Milton, Dryden, Pope;
Thou shalt not set up Wordsworth, Coleridge, Southey;
Because the first is crazed beyond all hope,
The second drunk, the third so quaint and mouthey ...
Thou shalt not bear false witness like the Blues ...
Thou shalt not write, in short, but what I choose.
This is true criticism, and you may kiss,
Exactly as you please, or not, the rod,
But if you don't, I'll lay it on, by God! (I.205-6)

... poetry ... is but passion,
Or at least was so ere it grew a fashion. (IV.106)

… Petrarch's self, if judged with due severity,
Is the Platonic pimp of all posterity.   (V.1)

John Keats … was killed off by one critique,
Just as he really promised something great …
'Tis strange the mind, that very fiery particle,
Should let itself be snuffed out by an article.   (XI.60)

But 'why then publish?' There are no rewards
Of fame or profit when the world grows weary.
I ask in turn why do you play at cards?
Why drink? Why read? To make some hour less
   dreary.   (XIV.11)

I rattle on exactly as I'd talk
With anybody in a ride or walk.   (XV.19)

No doubt if I had wished to pay my court
To critics or to hail the setting sun
Of tyranny of all kinds, my concision
Were more, but I was born for opposition.   (XV.22)

I say, in my slight way I may proceed
To play upon the surface of humanity.
I write the world nor care if the world read;
At least for this I cannot spare its vanity.
My Muse hath bred and still perhaps may breed
More foes by this same scroll. When I began it, I
Thought that it might turn out so; now I know it,
But still I am, or was, a pretty poet.   (XV.60)

Pleasure

My life here [at Cambridge] has been one continued routine of dissipation. *Letter to Elizabeth Pigot, 1807*

You cannot conceive what a delightful companion you are now you are gone. *Letter to Hobhouse, 1810*

I am learning Italian, and this day translated an ode of Horace ... I chatter with everybody, good or bad, and tradute prayers out of the mass ritual; but my lessons, though very long, are sadly interrupted by scamperings, and eating fruit, and peltings and playings; and I am in fact at school again, and make as little improvement now as I did then, my time wasted in the same way. *(Ib.)*

Anything to cure me of conjugating the accursed verb *'ennuyer'*. *Letter to Hodgson, 1811*

To me the most pleasing moments have generally been, when there is nothing more to be required; in short, the subsequent repose without satiety ... when you are secure of the past, yet without regret or disappointment. *Letter to Lady Melbourne, 1813*

A man may praise and praise, but no one recollects but that which pleases. *Letter to Moore, 1813*

The great object of life is sensation – to feel that we exist, even though in pain. It is this 'craving void' which drives us to gaming – to battle – to travel – to intemperate, but keenly felt pursuits of any description, whose principal attraction is the agitation inseparable from their accomplishment. *Letter to Annabella Milbanke, 1813*

A true voluptuary will never abandon his mind to the grossness of reality. It is by exalting the earthly, the material, the *physique* of our pleasures, by veiling these ideas, by forgetting them altogether, or, at least, never naming them hardly to one's self, that we alone can prevent them from disgusting. *Journal*, 1813

I have heard many a host libelled by his guests, with his burgundy yet reeking on their rascally lips. *(Ib.)*

I, who bear cold no better than an antelope, [have] never found a sun quite *done* to my taste. *(Ib.)*

I hate putting people into fusses, either with themselves or their favourites; it looks as if one did it on purpose. *(Ib.)*

I always begin the day with a bias towards going to parties; but, as the evening advances, my stimulus fails, and I hardly ever go out – and, when I do, always regret it. *(Ib.)*

I do not know that I am happiest when alone; but this I am sure of, that I never am long in the society even of *her* I love, (God knows too well, and the devil probably too,) without a yearning for the company of my lamp and my utterly confused and tumbled-over library. *(Ib.)*

The more violent the fatigue [from exercise], the better my spirits for the rest of the day; and then, my evenings have that calm nothingness of languor, which I most delight in. *(Ib.)*

Like other parties of the kind [a male drinking-bout], it was first silent, then talky, then argumentative, then disputatious, then unintelligible, then altogethery, then inarticulate, and then drunk … All was hiccup and happiness for the last hour or so. *Letter to Moore*, 1815

I dote upon ... the *patrician thoroughbred look*.

Diary, 1821

The only pleasure of fame is that it paves the way to pleasure; and the more intellectual our pleasure, the better for the pleasure and for us too.   (*Ib.*)

If we cannot contribute to make mankind more free and wise, we may amuse ourselves and those who like it.

Letter to Moore, 1821

I have a notion that Gamblers are as happy as most people, being always *excited*. Women, wine, fame, the table, even Ambition, *sate* now and then; but every turn of the card, and cast of the dice, keeps the Gamester alive: besides one can Game ten times longer than one can do any thing else.

Detached Thoughts, 1821

I doubt sometimes whether, after all, a quiet and unagitated life would have suited me: yet I sometimes long for it.   (*Ib.*)

Poverty is wretchedness; but it is perhaps to be preferred to the heartless unmeaning dissipation of the higher orders. I am thankful I am now clear of that, and my resolution to remain clear of it for the rest of my life is immutable.   *Conversation shortly before his death*

Don Juan

Oh pleasure, you're indeed a pleasant thing,
Although one must be damned for you no doubt.
I make a resolution every spring
Of reformation, ere the year run out,
But somehow this my vestal vow takes wing;
Yet still I trust it may be kept throughout.
I'm very sorry, very much ashamed,
And mean next winter to be quite reclaimed.   (I.119)

Man's a phenomenon, one knows not what,
And wonderful beyond all wondrous measure.
'Tis pity though in this sublime world that
Pleasure's a sin and sometimes sin's a pleasure.   (I.133)

'Tis pleasing to be schooled in a strange tongue
By female lips and eyes: that is, I mean,
When both the teacher and the taught are young …
                                        (II.164)

Man being reasonable must get drunk;
The best of life is but intoxication.
Glory, the grape, love, gold, in these are sunk
The hopes of all men and of every nation.   (II.179)

Though sages may pour out their wisdom's treasure,
There's no sterner moralist than pleasure.   (III.65)

… late hours, wine, and love are able
To do not much less damage than the table.   (III.66)

One of the two, according to your choice,
Woman or wine, you'll have to undergo.
Both maladies are taxes on our joys;
But which to choose, I really hardly know.   (IV.25)

'Tis pity wine should be so deleterious,
For tea and coffee leave us much more serious.   (IV.52)

A neat, snug study on a winter's night,
A book, friend, single lady, or a glass
Of claret, sandwich, and an appetite
Are things which make an English evening pass.   (V.58)

Let this one toil for bread, that rack for rent;
He who sleeps best may be the most content.   (IX.15)

Thrice happy they who have an occupation!   (XIV.77)

And hence high life is oft a dreary void,
A rack of pleasures, where we must invent
A something wherewithal to be annoyed …   (XIV.79)

*

I lived, I loved, I quaff'd, like thee:
I died: let earth my bones resign;
Fill up – thou canst not injure me;
The worm hath fouler lips than thine.

                    Inscription on his skull mug, 1808

Home & Abroad

How merrily we lives that travellers be! – if we had but food and raiment. But, in sober sadness, any thing is better than England, and I am infinitely amused with my pilgrimage as far as it has gone.   *Letter to Hodgson*, 1809

Intrigue here is the business of life ... If you make a proposal, which in England will bring a box on the ear from the meekest of virgins, to a Spanish girl, she thanks you for the honour you intend her, and replies, 'Wait till I am married, and I shall be too happy'.
     Letter to his mother, 1809

I like the Greeks, who are plausible rascals, – with all the Turkish vices, without their courage. However, some are brave, and all are beautiful, very much resembling the busts of Alcibiades; – the women not quite so handsome.
     Letter to Henry Drury, 1810

[The Turks] are extremely polite to strangers of any rank, properly protected; and as I have two servants and two soldiers, we get on with great *éclat*.   (*Ib.*)

I am like the Jolly Miller, caring for nobody, and not cared for. All countries are much the same in my eyes. I smoke, and stare at mountains, and twirl my mustachios very independently. I miss no comforts.   (*Ib.*)

I have nothing to request in England; everybody with whom I am at all connected seems asleep; as far as regards me, I shan't awake them.   *Letter to Hobhouse*, 1810

I have some idea of purchasing the Island of Ithaca.   (*Ib.*)

I am so convinced of the advantages of looking at mankind instead of reading about them, and the bitter effects of staying at home with all the narrow prejudices of an islander, that I think there should be a law amongst us, to set our young men abroad, for a term, among the few allies our wars have left us. *Letter to his mother*, 1811

I am growing *nervous* (how you will laugh!) – but it is true, – really, wretchedly, ridiculously, fine-ladically *nervous*. Your climate kills me; I can neither read, write, nor amuse myself, or any one else. My days are listless, and my nights restless; I have very seldom any society, and when I have, I run out of it. *Letter to Hodgson*, 1811 (back in England)

Give me a *sun*, I care not how hot, and sherbet, I care not how cool, and *my* Heaven is as easily made as your Persian's. *Letter to Moore*, 1813

Venice … has always been (next to the East) the greenest isle of my imagination. It has not disappointed me … I have been familiar with ruins too long to dislike desolation. *Letter to Moore*, 1816

I am a citizen of the world – all countries are alike to me. *Letter to Teresa Guiccioli*, 1819

Now what do you think of doing? I have two notions: one to visit England in the spring, the other to go to South America. Europe is grown decrepit; besides, it is all the same thing over again; those fellows are fresh as their world, and fierce as their earthquakes. *Letter to Hobhouse*, 1819

I am out of sorts, out of nerves; and now and then (I begin to fear) out of my senses. All this Italy has done for me, and not England: I defy all of you, and your climate to boot, to make me mad. But if ever I do really become a Bedlamite, and wear a strait waistcoat, let me be brought back among you; your people will then be proper company. *Letter to Murray*, 1819

The crown itself would not bribe me to return to England, unless business or actual urgency required it.

Letter to Hobhouse, 1820

I should like much to share some of your Champagne and La Fitte, but I am too Italian for Paris in general.

Letter to Moore, 1820

It is the custom [at Ravenna] … nobody fights, but they pop at you from behind trees, and put a knife into you in company, or in turning a corner, while you are blowing your nose.

Letter to Kinnaird, 1820

You must not trust Italian witnesses: nobody believes them in their own courts; why should you? For 50 or 100 Sequins you may have any testimony you please, and the Judge into the bargain.

Letter to Murray, 1820

My thoughts fail me when I must express myself in the effeminate words of the language of musicians.

Letter to Teresa Guiccioli, 1820

There is nothing like ridicule, the only weapon that the English climate cannot rust.

Letter to Kinnaird, 1820

No one was ever [popular] in Italy but an opera singer, or ever will be till the resurrection of Romulus.

(Ib.)

The Austrians … do not merit the name of Germans.

(Ib.)

You must not mind what the English fools say of Italy – they know nothing – they go gaping from Rome to Florence and so on – which is like seeing England – in Saint James's Street.

Letter to Lady Byron, 1820

An Italian winter is a sad thing … The air [is] replete with Scotticisms, which, though fine in the descriptions of Ossian, are somewhat tiresome in real, prosaic perspective.

Diary, 1821

In the fashionable world of London ... I [once] formed an item, a fraction, the segment of a circle, the unit of a million, the nothing of something.   *(Ib.)*

Whenever an American requests to see me (which is *not* unfrequently), I comply: 1stly, because I respect a people who acquired their freedom by firmness without excess; and 2ndly, because these trans-atlantic visits, 'few and far between', make me feel as if talking with Posterity from the other side of the Styx.   *(Ib.)*

Switzerland is a curst selfish, swinish country of brutes, placed in the most romantic region of the world.
Letter to Moore, 1821

All these American honours arise, perhaps, not so much from their enthusiasm for my 'Poeshie', as their belief in my dislike to the English, – in which I have the satisfaction to coincide with them. I would rather, however, have a nod from an American, than a snuff-box from an emperor.
*(Ib.*1822)

Alas! our dearly beloved countrymen have only discovered that they are tired, and not that they are tiresome.
Letter to Lord Blessington, 1823

My mother was Scotch, and my name and my family are both Norman; and as for myself, I am of no country.
Letter to the Count d'Orsay, 1823

Whoever goes into Greece at present should do it as Mrs. Fry went into Newgate – not in the expectation of meeting with any especial indication of existing probity, but in the hope that time and better treatment will reclaim the present burglarious and larcenous tendencies which have followed this General Gaol delivery.
Journal in Cephalonia, 1823

Don Juan

At leaving even the most unpleasant people
And places, one keeps looking at the steeple.   (II.14)

... Of late your scribblers think it worth
Their while to rear whole hotbeds in *their* works
Because one poet travelled 'mongst the Turks.   (V.42)

You are not a moral people, and you know it
Without the aid of too sincere a poet.   (XI.87; on the English)

... 'tis a low, newspaper, humdrum, lawsuit
Country ...   (XII.65; of England)

The English winter, ending in July
To recommence in August ...   (XIII.42)

An English autumn, though it hath no vines,
Blushing with bacchant coronals along
The paths, o'er which the far festoon entwines
The red grape in the sunny lands of song,
Hath yet a purchased choice of choicest wines:
The claret light and the madeira strong.
If Britain mourn her bleakness, we can tell her
The very best of vineyards is the cellar.   (XIII.76)

Society is now one polished horde,
Formed of two mighty tribes, the Bores and
    Bored.   (XIII.95)

For ennui is a growth of English root,
Though nameless in our language. We retort
The fact for words and let the French translate
That awful yawn which sleep cannot abate.   (XIII.101)

A fox-hunt to a foreigner is strange;
'Tis also subject to the double danger
Of tumbling first and having in exchange
Some pleasant jesting at the awkward stranger.   (XIV.32)

... he had, like Alcibiades,
The art of living in all climes with ease.   (XV.11)

Ageing & Death

There is to me something so incomprehensible in death, that I can neither speak nor think on the subject. Indeed, when I looked on the mass of corruption which was the being from whence I sprung, I doubted within myself whether I *was*, or whether she *was not*. I have lost her who gave me being, and some of those who made that being a blessing. I have neither hopes nor fears beyond the grave.
Letter to Hobhouse, 1811 (on the death of his mother)

Five and twenty is almost too late in life for anything but the Senate, or the Church.   *(Ib.)*

Peace be with the dead! Regret cannot wake them. With a sigh to the departed, let us resume the dull business of life, in the certainty that we also shall have our respose.
Letter to R.C. Dallas, 1811

Is there any thing in the future that can possibly console us for not being always *twenty-five*?   *Journal*, 1813

I have now and then fits of giddiness, and deafness, which make me think like Swift – that I shall be like him and the *withered* tree he saw – which occasioned the reflection and 'die at top' first.   *Letter to his half-sister*, 1816

To be tiresome is the privilege of old age and absence; I avail myself of the latter, and the former I have anticipated.
Letter to Moore, 1816

The time is past in which I could feel for the dead ... 'I have supped full of horrors', and events of this kind [the death of Lady Melbourne] leave only a kind of numbness worse than pain, – like a violent blow on the elbow, or on the head.   *Letter to Murray*, 1818

'*Implora pace*'. I hope, whoever may survive me, and shall see me put in the foreigners' burying-ground at the Lido, within the fortress by the Adriatic, will see those two words, and no more, put over me. I trust they won't think of 'pickling, and bringing me home to Clod or Blunderbuss Hall'. I am sure my bones would not rest in an English grave, or my clay mix with the earth of that country. I believe the thought would drive me mad on my deathbed.   (*Ib.*1819)

My time has been passed viciously and agreeably; at thirty-one so few years, months, days, remain, that 'Carpe diem' is not enough. I have been obliged to crop even the seconds, for who can trust to-morrow? – to-morrow quotha? to-hour, to-minute ...   *Letter to Hobhouse*, 1819

You speak of [my mother-in-law's] illness: she is not of those who die: – the amiable only do; and those whose death would *do good* live.   *Letter to Murray*, 1820

A man always *looks dead* after his Life has appeared, and I should certes not survive the appearance of mine.
                                             Letter to Moore, 1821

I do not dread idiotism or madness so much as [Swift] did. On the contrary, I think some quieter stages of both must be preferable to much of what men think the possession of their senses.   *Diary*, 1821

At twelve o' the clock, midnight, *i.e.* in twelve minutes, I shall have completed thirty and three years of age!!! – and I go to my bed with a heaviness of heart at having lived so long, and to so little purpose.   (*Ib.*)

I do not think I am so much *ennuyé* as I was at nineteen. The proof is that then I must game, or drink, or be in motion of some kind, or I was miserable. At present, I can mope in quietness ... What I feel most growing upon me are laziness, and a disrelish more powerful than indifference.   (*Ib.*)

It is singular how soon we lose the impression of what ceases to be *constantly* before us ... I except indeed our recollections of Womankind: there is no forgetting *them*.
Detached Thoughts, 1821

It was one of the deadliest and heaviest feelings of my life to feel that I was no longer a boy. From that moment I began to grow old in my own esteem; and in my esteem age is not estimable. *(Ib.)*

I have written my memoirs, but omitted *all* the really *consequential* and *important* parts, from deference to the dead, to the living, and to those who must be both. *(Ib.)*

I was a fool then [when an adolescent], and am not much wiser now. *(Ib.)*

Let me not live to be old: give me youth, which is the fever of reason, and not age, which is the palsy. I remember my youth, when my heart overflowed with affection towards all who showed any symptoms of liking towards me; and now, at thirty-six, no very advanced period of life, I can scarcely, by raking up the dying embers of affection in that same heart, excite even a temporary flame to warm my chilled feelings. *Conversation with Lady Blessington*, 1823

Do you suppose that I wish for life? I have grown heartily sick of it, and shall welcome the hour I depart from it. Why should I regret it? Can it afford me any pleasure? ... Few men can live faster than I did. I am, literally speaking, a young old man. Hardly arrived at manhood, I had attained the zenith of fame. Pleasure I have known under every form it can present itself to mortals. I have travelled, satisfied my curiosity, lost every illusion ... But the apprehension of two things now haunts my mind. I picture myself slowly expiring on a bed of torture, or terminating my days like Swift – a grinning idiot! Would to Heaven the day were arrived in which, rushing, sword in hand, on a body of Turks, and fighting like one weary of existence, I shall meet immediate, painless death.
To his doctor, shortly before his last illness.

Forward! Courage! Follow my example! Don't be afraid!
Among his purported last words

Don Juan

… now at thirty years my hair is grey
(I wonder what it will be like at forty?
I thought of a peruke the other day);
My heart is not much greener, and in short I
Have squandered my whole summer while 'twas May.
And feel no more the spirit to retort. I
Have spent my life, both interest and principal,
And deem not, what I deemed, my soul invincible.   (I.213)

My days of love are over, me no more
The charms of maid, wife, and still less of widow
Can make the fool of which they made before;
In short, I must not lead the life I did do.   (I.216)

So for a good old-gentlemanly vice,
I think I must take up with avarice.   (*Ib.*)

What is the end of fame? 'Tis but to fill
A certain portion of uncertain paper.
Some like it to climbing up a hill,
Whose summit, like all hills, is lost in vapour.
For this men write, speak, preach, and heroes kill,
And bards burn what they call their midnight taper,
To have when the original is dust,
A name, a wretched picture, and worse bust.   (I.218)

Well – well, the world must turn upon its axis,
And all mankind turn with it, heads or tails,
And live and die, make love and pay our taxes
And as the veering wind shifts, shift our sails.   (II.4)

As for the ladies, I have nought to say,
A wanderer from the British world of fashion,
Where I, like other 'dogs have had my day',
Like other men too, may have had my passion,
But that, like other things, has passed away,
And all her fools whom I *could* lay the lash on,
Foes, friends, men, women, now are nought to me
But dreams of what has been, no more to be.   (II.166)

'Whom the gods love die young' was said of yore,
And many deaths do they escape by this:
The death of friends and that which slays even more,
The death of friendship, love, youth, all that is,
Except mere breath. And since the silent shore
Awaits at last even those whom longest miss
The old archer's shafts, perhaps the early grave,
Which men weep over, may be meant to save.   (IV.12)

Of all the barbarous Middle Ages, that
Which is the most barbarous is the middle age
Of man …
Too old for youth, too young at thirty-five
To herd with boys or hoard with good threescore.
I wonder people should be left alive,
But since they are, that epoch is a bore.   (XII.1–2)

I know that some would fain postpone this era,
Reluctant as all placemen to resign
Their post, but theirs is merely a chimera,
For they have passed life's equinoctial line.
But then they have their claret and madeira
To irrigate the dryness of decline,
And country meetings and the Parliament
And debt and what not for their solace sent.   (XIII.5)

Death, so called, is a thing which makes men weep,
And yet a third of life is passed in sleep.   (XIV.3)

In youth I wrote because my mind was full,
And now because I feel it growing dull.   (XIV.10)

The Byronic Self

I will cut myself a path through the world or perish in the attempt ... I will carve myself the passage to Grandeur, but never with Dishonour.   *Letter to his mother, 1804*

I am a very unlucky fellow, for I think I had naturally not a bad heart; but it has been so bent, twisted, and trampled on, that it has now become as hard as a Highlander's heelpiece.   *Letter to his half-sister, 1808*

Mismanagement is the hereditary epidemic of [the Byron] brood.   *Letter to Hobhouse, 1811*

I am the very worst companion for young people in the world.   *Letter to Dallas, 1811*

I am indeed very wretched, and like all complaining persons I can't help telling you so.
          Letter to Hobhouse, 1811

I never risk *rivalry* in anything.
          Letter to Lady Melbourne, 1812

My correspondence since I was sixteen has not been of a nature to allow of any trust except to a lock and key.   *(Ib.)*

Was there ever such a slave to impulse?   *(Ib.1813)*

The reputation of 'gloom', if one's friends are not included in the *reputants*, is of great service; as it saves one from a legion of impertinents, in the shape of common-place acquaintance. But thou know'st I can be a right merry and conceited fellow, and rarely *larmoyant*.
          Letter to Moore, 1813

I look upon myself as a very facetious personage ...
Nobody laughs more, and though your friend Joanna
Baillie says somewhere that 'Laughter is the child of
misery', I do not believe her (unless indeed in a hysteric),
tho' I think it is sometimes the parent.

Letter to Annabella Milbanke, 1813

Whatever I may, and have, or shall feel, I have that within
me, that bounds against opposition. I have *quick feelings*,
and not very *good nerves*.   *Letter to Lady Melbourne, 1814*

There are three things I can do which you cannot. I can
swim across that river – I can snuff out that candle at the
distance of twenty paces – and I have written a poem of
which fourteen thousand copies were sold in one day.

Conversation with Dr John Polidori, 1816

If I live ten years longer, you will see, however, that it is not
over with me – I don't mean in literature, for that is
nothing; and it may seem odd enough to say, I do not think
it my vocation. But you will see that I shall do something or
other – the times and fortune permitting – that, 'like the
cosmogony, or creation of the world, will puzzle the
philosophers of all ages'.   *Letter to Moore, 1817*

I mean to be as mercenary as possible, an example ...
which I should have followed in my youth, and I might still
have been a prosperous gentleman.

Letter to Murray, 1817

So altered since last year his pen is,
I think he's lost his wits at Venice,
Or drained his brains away as stallion
To some dark-eyed and warm Italian.   *(Ib.)*

I shall make what I can of the remainder of my youth,
and confess, that, like Augustus, I would rather die
standing.   *(Ib.)*

I am only a spectator upon earth, till a tenfold opportunity
offers. It may come yet.   *Letter to Moore, 1818*

I prefer a private life, and have lived almost entirely with
my paramour, her husband, *his* son by a former marriage,
and her father, with her confidante.

Letter to Hobhouse, 1819

That lust for duelling of which you used to accuse me …
has long subsided into a moderate desire of killing one's
more personal enemies.   *(Ib.)*

It is very iniquitous to make me pay my debts – you have
no idea of the pain it gives me.   *Letter to Kinnaird, 1819*

I have been more ravished myself than any body since the
Trojan war.   *Letter to Hoppner, 1819*

I have settled into regular *serventismo* … I double a shawl
with considerable alacrity; but have not yet arrived at the
perfection of putting it on the right way.
                                   Letter to Hobhouse, 1820

Brummel at Calais, Scrope at Bruges, Buonaparte at St.
Helena … and I at Ravenna, only think! So many great
men! There has been nothing like it since Themistocles at
Magnesia, and Marius at Carthage.   *(Ib.)*

Why, I do like one or two vices, to be sure; but I can back a
horse and fire a pistol 'without winking or blinking' like
Major Sturgeon; I have fed at times for two months
together on *sheer biscuit and water* (without metaphor); I can
get over seventy or eighty miles a day *riding* post upon [?]
of all sorts, and *swim five* at a Stretch, taking a *piece* before
and after, as at Venice, in 1818, or at least I *could do*, and
have done it ONCE, and I never was ten minutes in my life
over a *solitary* dinner.   *Letter to Murray, 1820*

I was always violent.   *Detached Thoughts, 1821*

The way to be immortal (I mean *not* to die at all) is to have
me for your heir. I recommend you to put me in your will;
and you will see that (as long as *I* live at least) you will
never even catch cold.   *Letter to Kinnaird, 1821*

I am not sure that long life is desirable for one of my temper
and constitutional depression of Spirits, which of course I
suppress in society; but which breaks out when alone, and
in my writings, in spite of myself.   *Letter to Murray, 1821*

I … believe in predestination, … and in the depravity of the
human heart in general, and of my own in particular.
                        Conversation with Lady Blessington, 1823

As for personal safety, besides that it ought not to be a
consideration, I take it that a man is on the whole as safe in
one place as another; and, after all, he had better end with
a bullet than bark in his body. If we are not taken off with
the sword, we are like to march off with an ague in this
mud basket [Missolonghi]; and to conclude with a very bad
pun, to the ear rather than to the eye, better *martially* than
marsh-ally.   *Letter to Charles Hancock*, 1824

Don Juan

He had travelled 'mongst the Arabs, Turks, and Franks
And knew the self-loves of the different nations,
And having lived with people of all ranks,
Had something ready upon most occasions …
'Twas all the same to him – 'God save the king'
Or 'Ça ira' according to the fashion all.
His Muse made increment of anything
From the high lyric down to the low rational …   (III.84–5)

As a boy, I thought myself a clever fellow
And wished that others held the same opinion;
They took it up when my days grew more mellow,
And other minds acknowledged my dominion.   (IV.3)

Some have accused me of a strange design
Against the creed and morals of the land
And trace it in this poem every line.
I don't pretend that I quite understand
My own meaning when I would be very fine;
But the fact is that I have nothing planned,
Unless it were to be a moment merry,
A novel word in my vocabulary.   (IV.5)

What, can I prove a lion then no more?
A ballroom bard, a foolscap, hot-press darling? …
Why then I'll swear, as poet Wordy swore
(Because the world won't read him, always snarling),
That taste is gone, that fame is but a lottery,
Drawn by the bluecoat misses of a coterie.   (IV.109)

I think I should have made a decent spouse
If I had never proved the soft condition.
I think I should have made monastic vows
But for my peculiar superstition.
'Gainst rhyme I never should have knocked my brows
Nor broken my own head nor that of Priscian
Nor worn the motley mantle of a poet
If someone had not told me to forego it.   (XV.24)

*

Now, I'll put out my taper
(I've finished my paper
For these stanzas you see on the *brink* stand)
There's a whore on my right
For I rhyme best at Night
When a C—t is tied close to *my Inkstand.*

It was Mahomet's notion
That comical motion   (see Gibbon)
Increased his 'devotion in prayer' –
If that tenet holds good
In a Prophet, it should
In a poet be equally fair. –

For, in rhyme or in love
(Which both come from above)
I'll *stand* with our '*Tommy*' or '*Sammy*' ('Moore'
    and 'Rogers')
But the Sopha and lady
Are both of them ready
And so, here's 'Good Night to you dammee!'

Letter to Murray, 1818